MW01222713

Continents
EUROPE

Edited by: Pallabi B. Tomar, Hitesh Iplani
Managing editor: Tapasi De
Designed by: Vijesh Chahal, Anil Kumar, Rohit Kumar
Illustrated by: Suman S. Roy, Tanoy Choudhury
Colouring done by: Vinay Kumar, Kiran Kumari & Pradeep Kumar

CONTENTS

Introduction

Europe is the second smallest and the sixth largest continent on Earth. It is a vast peninsula of the great **Eurasian** land mass. (Asia and Europe do not have a dividing water body; they are a continuous mass of land. This land mass is known as Eurasia.)

Location

In the east, Europe is separated from Asia by the Ural Mountains and the Ural River. In the southeast, Caspian Sea and the Caucasus mountain range separates it from Asia. The Black Sea, the Bosporus Strait, the Sea of Marmara, and the Dardanelles Strait mark its boundary in the south. It is separated from the African continent by the Mediterranean Sea and the Strait of Gibraltar. Europe has Arctic Ocean in the north and the Atlantic Ocean in the west. The North Sea and the Baltic Sea are connected to the Atlantic Ocean.

Covering about 2 per cent of the Earth's surface and about 6.8 per cent of its land area Europe has approximately 50 states. Europe is the third most populated continent after Asia and Africa. It accounts for about 11 per cent of the world population.

List of European countries

	Flag	Name	Capital	Currency	Official Language
1.		Albania	Tirana	Lek	Albanian
2.		Andorra	Andorra la Vella	Euro	Catalan
3.		Armenia	Yerevan	Drams	Armenian
4.		Austria	Vienna	Euro	German
5.		Azerbaijan	Baku	Manat	Azerbaijani
6.		Belarus	Minsk	Belarusian rouble	Belarusian
7.		Belgium	Brussels	Euro	Dutch, French, German
8.		Bosnia and Herzegovina	Sarajevo	Konvertibilna markas (BAM)	Bosnian, Croatian
9.		Bulgaria	Sofia	Bulgarian Lev	Bulgarian
10.		Croatia	Zagreb	Croatian Kuna	Croatian
11.		Cyprus	Nicosia	Euro	Greek, Turkish
12.		Czech Republic	Prague	Czech koruna	Czech Slovak
13.		Denmark	Copenhagen	Danish kroner	Danish, Faroese, Greenlandic
14.		Estonia	Tallinn	Euro	Estonian
15.		Finland	Helsinki	Euro	Finnish, Swedish
16.		France	Paris	Euro	French
17.		Georgia	Tbilisi	Lari	Georgian
18.		Germany	Berlin	Euro	German

19.	Greece	Athens	Euro	Greek
20.	Hungary	Budapest	Forints	Hungarian
21.	Iceland	Reykjavík	Icelandic krona	Icelandic
22.	Ireland	Dublin	Euro	English
23.	Italy	Rome	Euro	Italian
24.	Kazakhstan	Astana	Tenge	Kazakh
25.	Latvia	Riga	Lats	Latvian
26.	Liechtenstein	Vaduz	Swiss francs	German
27.	Lithuania	Vilnius	Litas	Lithuanian
28.	Luxembourg	Luxembourg City	Euro	Luxembourgish, German, French
29.	Macedonia	Skopje	Macedonian denars	Macedonian, Albanian
30.	Malta	Valletta	Euro	Maltese, English
31.	Moldova	Chisinau	Moldovan lei	Moldovan
32.	Monaco	Monaco	Euro	French
33.	Montenegro	Podgorica	Euro	Montenegrin
34.	Netherlands	Amsterdam (capital)	Euro	Dutch, Frisian
35.	Norway	Oslo	Norwegian kroner	Bokmal Norwegian, Nynorsk Norwegian
36.	Poland	Warsaw	Zloty	Polish
37.	Portugal	Lisbon	Euro	Portuguese, Mirandese
38.	Romania	Bucharest	Lei	Romanian

39.		Russia	Moscow	Russian roubles	Russian
40.		San Marino	City of San Marino	Euro	Italian
41.		Serbia	Belgrade	Serbian dinars	Serbian
42.		Slovakia	Bratislava	Euro	Slovak
43.		Slovenia	Ljubljana	Euro	Slovenian, Italian
44.		Spain	Madrid	Euro	Castilian Spanish
45.		Sweden	Stockholm	Swedish kronor	Swedish
46.		Switzerland	Bern or Berne	Swiss francs	German, French, Italian
47.		Turkey	Ankara	Turkish liras	Turkish
48.		Ukraine	Kiev	Hryvnia	Ukrainian
49.		United Kingdom	London	British pounds	English
50.		Vatican City	Vatican City	Euro	No official language; Italian is used for most purposes.

Europe at a glance

The Ancient Greece in Europe is regarded as the birthplace of Western culture. Both the Greek and the Roman civilizations flourished here. Western culture has deeply influenced the present day world through its philosophies, arts, empires and revolutions. However, the history of the continent is filled with numerous internal wars, the fall of colonial empires, etc.

The most widely spoken languages are Russian, German, English, French and Italian. Some countries have more than one official language.

Size	10, 180, 000 sq. Km
Population	731, 000, 000
Number of countries	50
Highest point	Mt. Elbrus (5,633 m) in the Alps
Lowest point	Caspian Sea (28 m below sea level)

History

The beginnings of civilization in ancient Europe are not as old as the civilizations of Mesopotamia and Egypt. The Roman and the Greek cultures flourished in Europe. Ancient Greek culture, thought and philosophy had a huge influence on the Western civilization.

The concept of democratic government and individual-centric cultures are often attributed to Ancient Greece. Greece is known as the birthplace of democracy.

The Greeks invented the **polis** or **city-state**, which played an important role in the formation of the concepts of modern administrative bodies.

After the gradual decline of the Roman Empire, Europe entered the **Middle Ages**. The period saw a continuation of trends begun during late classical age, including decline in population, a decline in trade, and increased migration. This period is also called the **Dark Ages**.

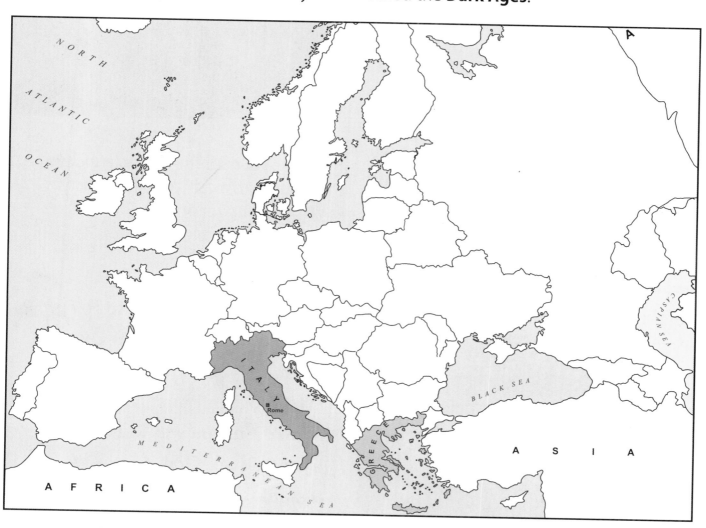

Dark Ages

Dark Ages is a term referring to the period of cultural and economic decline that occurred in Europe following the decline of the Roman Empire. It is known as a period of lack of intellectual and creative talent. The term Dark Age was first used by the Italian scholar and poet Petrarch in the 1330s.

Crusades

The Crusades were a series of religious wars waged by most of the Roman Catholic Europe, particularly the Franks of France and the Holy Roman Empire. These holy wars were fought over a period of nearly 200 years!

Other campaigns in Spain and Eastern Europe continued into the 15th century. The Crusades were fought mainly by Roman Catholic forces against Muslims who had occupied the near east. Orthodox Christians also took part in fighting against Islamic forces in some Crusades.

The Crusades originally had the goal of recapturing Jerusalem the Holy Land

Crusades

from Muslim rule. They were launched in response to a call from the Christian Byzantine Empire for help against the expansion of the Muslim Seljuk Turks into Anatolia.

Crusades

The name Europe is said to have come from ancient Greek mythology. In ancient Greek mythology, a Phoenician princess named Europa was kidnapped by the Greek God Zeus after assuming the form of a white bull.

Black Death

The Black Death was a plague that killed one third of the European population. It began in 1347 and ended in 1350. This is the most famous plague in the history of Europe since it killed so many people.

technology, philosophy, political concepts and the Christian religion to spread throughout the world. It was called **Colonialism**.

Colonialism was the exploitation of a weaker country by a stronger country usually for land, labour and other useful resources.

The period of dark ages was followed by the **Renaissance** or reawakening as some scholars call it. The Renaissance was a period of discovery, exploration and increase in scientific knowledge.

With the passage of time a new concept cropped up. It helped the European civilization—its language,

Renaissance

Renaissance is an Italian word which means 'rebirth'.

Portugal, Spain, France, Netherlands and the United Kingdom started building large colonial empires with vast holdings in Africa, the Americas and Asia.

Jomes Watt

With the dawning age of the age of discovery, the ideas of democracy started taking hold on Europe. Struggles for independence arose, most notably in France which finally led to the **French Revolution**. This led to vast upheavals in Europe as these revolutionary ideas were propagated across the continent. Slowly all the colonies gained their independence and colonialism came to an end.

With the invention of the steam engine by James Watt the Industrial Revolution started in the United Kingdom in the late 18th century, leading to a move away from agriculture. This gradually spread to the whole of Europe.

Many of the states in Europe took their present form as a result of World War I.

From the end of World War II till the end of the Cold War, Europe was divided into two major political and economic blocks—Communist nations in Eastern Europe and capitalist countries in Western Europe. Around 1990, with the fall of the Berlin Wall, the Eastern bloc disintegrated.

Steam engine developed by Jomes Watt.

Geography of Europe

Europe can be divided into seven geographic regions: **Scandinavia** (Iceland, Norway, Sweden, Finland, and Denmark); **the British Isles** (the United Kingdom and Ireland); **W. Europe** (France, Belgium, the Netherlands, Luxembourg, and Monaco); **S. Europe** (Portugal, Spain, Andorra, Italy, Malta, San Marino, and Vatican City); **Central Europe** (Germany, Switzerland, Liechtenstein, Austria, Poland, the Czech Republic, Slovakia, and Hungary); **SE Europe** (Slovenia, Croatia, Bosnia and Herzegovina, Serbia, Montenegro, Albania, Macedonia, Romania, Bulgaria, Greece, and the European part of Turkey); and **E. Europe** (Estonia, Latvia, Lithuania, Belarus, Ukraine, Moldova, the European portion of Russia, and the countries of Georgia, Armenia, and Azerbaijan).

Northern Norway, Sweden, Finland, and Russia lie within the Arctic Circle. The prime meridian (0° longitude) runs through Great Britain, France and Spain.

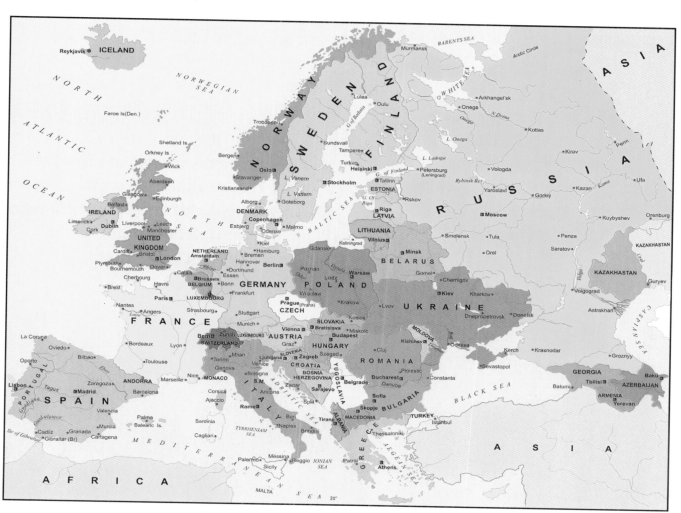

When the great land masses of Africa and India collided with Europe and Asia, about 100 million years ago they caused the crust of the Earth to crumple upwards in a long almost continuous ridge of high ground. It stretches from the Alps, through Turkey, Iran and Afghanistan to the Himalayas.

The coast of Europe about 40,000 km long, is extremely irregular and dotted with many islands. Major islands include— Iceland, the British Isles, Novaya Zemlya, Franz Josef Land, Svalbard the Balearic Islands, Corsica, Sardinia, Sicily, Malta and Crete.

Europe is a collection of connected peninsulas and nearby islands. The two largest peninsulas are 'mainland' Europe and Scandinavia to the north, divided from each other by the Baltic Sea. Three smaller peninsulas—Iberia, Italy and the Balkans, emerge from the southern margin of the mainland. The Balkan Peninsula is separated from Asia by the Black and Aegean Seas. Italy is separated from the Balkans by the Adriatic Sea and from Iberia by the Mediterranean Sea, which also separates Europe from Africa. Eastward, mainland Europe widens much like the mouth of a funnel, until the boundary with Asia is reached at the Ural Mountains and Ural River, the Caspian Sea and the Caucasus Mountains.

Land

The landscape of Europe shows great variation within small areas. The southern regions are mountainous, while moving north the terrain descends from the high Alps, through hilly uplands into broad, low northern plains, which are vast in the east. An arc of uplands also exists along the north-western seaboard, beginning in the western British Isles and continuing along the mountainous, fjord-cut spine of Norway.

Europe can be divided into four main regions. They are, (from north to south) the **Northern Highlands**, the **Great European Plain**, the **Central Highlands** and the **Alpine Mountains**.

Ural Mountains

Mt. Blanc

The Central Highlands, extending east-west across central Europe, are moderately high and heavily wooded. Examples of these highlands are the Massif Central and the Vosges of France, the Ardennes of Belgium, the Black Forest and Taunus Mountains of Germany, and the Ore and Sudeten mountains on the Czech Republic's northern border. Except in such large river valleys as those of the Rhine, Rhône, Elbe and Danube, the Central Highlands are sparsely settled.

The Northern Highlands, which include the mountains of Scandinavia and of the northern British Isles, were once overrun by huge glaciers. The glaciers left many lakes, rounded mountains and U-shaped valleys. The highest point, Galdhöpiggen, in Norway, is more than 2,400 m above sea level.

The Great European Plain extends from south-western France to the Ural Mountains in Russia. It includes northern France, south-eastern Great Britain, most of Belgium and the Netherlands, Denmark, northern Germany and southern Sweden. Much of Europe's population and industry and many of the continent's major cities, are located on this plain.

The Alpine Mountains extend across southern Europe from Spain to southern Russia. Among these mountains are the Sierra Nevada, Pyrenees, Alps, Pindus, Balkan and Caucasus mountains. These are high, rugged ranges with steep slopes.

The huge Alpine mountain chain, of which the Pyrenees, the Alps, the Carpathians, the Balkans and the Caucasus are the principal links, traverses the continent from west to east. The highest points are Mt. Elbrus (5,633 m) in the Caucasus and Mont Blanc (4,807 m) in the Alps.

Mt. Elbrus

Lake Ladoga

Rivers and lakes

Rivers are of great economic importance in Europe because many of them provide navigation and large amounts of water power. Most European rivers are quite short. The Volga River, the continent's longest river, is 3,685 km in length, about the same length as the Mississippi River.

Other large southward flowing rivers include the Dnieper, Danube, Don, Po, Rhône and Ebro. Among the northward-flowing rivers are the Loire, Seine, Rhine, Elbe, Oder, Vistula, Western Dvina, Northern Dvina and Pechora.

Most of Europe's lakes are in the north. Finland is the chief lake country; about 9 per cent of its area is water. Lakes Ladoga and Onega, in Russia, are Europe's largest lakes. Other large lakes include Lakes Vänern and Vättern in Sweden and Lake Balaton in Hungary. Many of the Alpine lakes of central Europe are popular tourist attractions. Among the largest of these are Lakes Geneva and Constance, both on the Swiss border.

Rhine

Plants and animals

The far north is a treeless region where only small mosses, lichens and ferns can withstand the cold winters. South of this region is a coniferous forest of pine, spruce, fir, and larch that stretches across northern Europe. Below this is a mixture of coniferous and broadleaf (deciduous) forests, which include beech, ash, oak, hazel, poplar and willow trees. Broadleaf forests occur mainly in a belt stretching north-eastward from Portugal to Denmark.

The plants that border the Mediterranean Sea are mainly small, drought-resistant southern evergreens. The chief trees include Aleppo pine and

Brown bear

cypress, cork oak, and Spanish chestnut. On the dry steppes of Spain and south-eastern Europe, grasses make up most of the natural vegetation.

Since the land has been densely populated for centuries, wildlife has been greatly reduced. The European bison, for example, is almost extinct. Among the remaining larger wild animals are the brown bear, deer and the elk. Smaller animals include the badger, beaver, chamois, chipmunk, fox, genet, hedgehog, lynx, marmot, marten, mole, otter, polecat, porcupine, rabbit, squirrel, weasel, wildcat, wild pig, wolf and wolverine. Europe has few snakes.

Thrushes, finches, warblers and buntings are probably the most commonly found birds. Others include the raven, rook, jackdaw, magpie, nutcracker, woodpecker, cuckoo, kingfisher, swift, falcon, hawk and eagle.

Climate

Despite Europe's northerly location, much of the continent has an agreeable climate. This is largely due to the temperate influence of the ocean and seas. Of all of Europe's advantages, none stand out as much as Europe's mild and temperate climate. Winters in Madrid and Paris are less severe than those in New York and Boston.

The reasons for Europe's mild climate are due to two factors— prevailing westerly winds and the North Atlantic Drift Ocean current. All of Europe is subject to the moderating influence of prevailing westerly winds from the Atlantic Ocean.

All months have average temperatures. Summers are cool and winters are mild. Rain falls during all months and snow is uncommon. Humidity is high; there are many foggy days; and the sky is often cloudy.

In central and eastern Europe, where the ocean's influence is less, the climate is largely continental. The region heats up quickly in summer and cools down quickly in winter. Summers vary from warm to hot. Winters are cold. Compared with the marine climate, the continent has less rainfall (coming largely in summer), more snow and fewer cloudy days.

WINTER SEA ICE COVER

NORTH ATLANTIC DRIFT

GULF STREAM

NAOW

Southern Europe has a Mediterranean climate. Summers are hot and dry. Winters are rainy and mild even though light snows and freezing temperatures may occur. Sub polar and tundra climates, with extremely long, cold winters, are found in the far north.

A semiarid climate is found in small regions of central Spain and near the Caspian Sea. These dry regions receive only enough rain to grow small plants. There are no true deserts in Europe.

The Gulf Stream is nicknamed 'Europe's central heating', because it makes Europe's climate warmer and wetter than it would otherwise be.

The climate is strongly conditioned by the Gulf Stream, which warms the western region to levels unattainable at similar latitudes on other continents.

As far as rainfall is concerned, most parts of Europe receive an annual rainfall of 20-60 inches, with the maximum of it happening towards the West of the mountains (around 80 inches in general). The areas receiving lighter rainfall include the Southern part of Spain, Kazakhstan and northern part of Scandinavia.

The European Union

The European Union (EU) is an economic and political union of 27 member states: Austria, Belgium, Bulgaria, Cyprus, the Czech Republic, Denmark, Estonia, Finland, France, Germany, Greece, Hungary, Italy, Latvia, Lithuania, Luxembourg, Malta, the Netherlands, Poland, Portugal, Republic of Ireland, Romania, Slovakia, Slovenia, Spain, Sweden and the United Kingdom. The Union's membership has grown from the original six founding states—Belgium, France, (then-West) Germany, Italy, Luxembourg and the Netherlands which are located primarily in Europe.

The EU traces its origins from the European Coal and Steel Community (ECSC) and the European Economic Community (EEC) formed by six countries in 1948. The Maastricht Treaty established

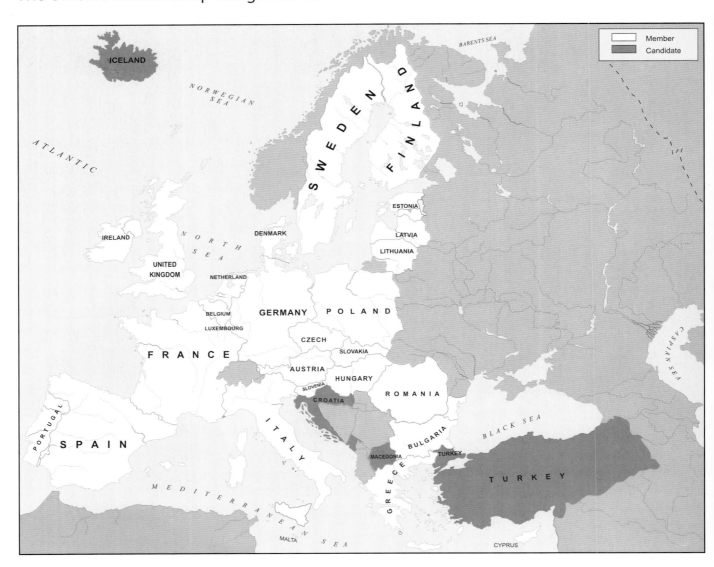

The European Union flag

the European Union under its current name in 1993. The European Union (EU) was founded in the aftermath of World War II to promote stability and economic cooperation between member states.

Important institutions of the EU include the European Commission, the Council of the European Union, the European Council, the Court of Justice of the European Union and the European Central Bank. The European Parliament is elected every five years by EU citizens.

On 1 December, 2009, the Lisbon Treaty created a permanent President of the European Council, the first of which is Herman Van Rompuy.

The political shape of Europe was dramatically changed when the Berlin Wall fell in 1989. This led to the unification of Germany in October 1990 and the coming of democracy to the countries of central and Eastern Europe as they broke away from Soviet Russian control.

The European Union flag

The flag is blue in colour with 12 five-pointed gold stars arranged in a circle in the centre. Blue represents the sky of the Western world, the stars are the peoples of Europe in a circle— a symbol of unity. The number of stars has nothing to do with the number of members countries. The number of stars is fixed.

The **euro** (symbol- €) is the single currency of the European Union.

Religion

Jesus Christ

Christianity has been practiced in Europe since the 1st century. In 301 AD, the Kingdom of Armenia became the first country to establish Christianity as its state religion. Soon after, the Roman Empire officially adopted Christianity in AD 380. Judaism is the largest non-Christian religion. Jews live mainly in the large cities. Muslims are concentrated in parts of the southeast, particularly in Bosnia and Herzegovina, Albania, Turkey and Azerbaijan.

Religion in Europe has been a major influence on art, culture, philosophy and law. The largest religion in Europe for at least a millennium and a half has been Christianity.

Two countries in South-eastern Europe have Muslim majorities. Smaller religions include Judaism, Buddhism, Sikhism and Hinduism which are found in their largest groups in Britain and France.

Symbols of Judaism

Gautam Buddha

20

Festivals of Europe

The Redentore Festival

There are many European festivals which are famous worldwide. Some of them are:

The Redentore Festival: Celebrated in Venice, the Redentore festival is marked with fun, feast and festivities. It is celebrated on the third Sunday of every July, this is one of the most beautiful and spectacular festivals of Europe.

Tomatina Festival: This is the festival wherein you get to throw tomatoes at anyone and everyone present even in the farthest range of your throwing power! It is a part of the larger Bunol parties that take place in Spain towards the end of August.

Edinburgh Festival: For the experts of art, this festival is a favourite. This festival features some of the best fine arts in the whole of Europe. It attracts a huge crowd consisting of artists, collectors and onlookers.

Ghent Festival: It is the largest open air and cultural festival in Europe and takes place at Ghent towards the end of July.

Tomatina Festival

Important cities of Europe

Louvre Museum

Cathedral Notre-Dame

No visit to France is complete without stopping by the Cathedral Notre-Dame. History buffs will enjoy the rich history of this attraction while art lovers will enjoy the beautiful statues, columns and windows.

Paris

Paris is one of the world's most vibrant and cultured cities. It is the most romantic city in Europe and also called the city of love. Everyone will enjoy a boat trip on the River Seine where you can sightsee all the main buildings of Paris. The Eiffel Tower can be called 'the symbol of Paris' and is the most famous sight on a boat trip. Paris offers a lot of attractions including the Notre Dame Cathedral, the Louvre Museum, Montmartre and Place de la Concorde. Paris is also famous for its wine and awesome perfumes.

Europe fetches the maximum number of tourists in a year due to its warm people and great natural beauty, coupled with aesthetic modernity. It is a well-known fact that almost each and every country that comes under the European region has major tourist hubs, which attract tourists from all over the world. Not only people from other continents, but people from within Europe also travel to the various tourist destinations in Europe.

Eiffel Tower

Known as one of the most famous landmarks in the world, there is no structure that has ever been built like the Eiffel Tower. The tower is 299.9 m high and one of the tallest buildings in the world. The view of Paris from the tower is definitely a must see if you are in Paris.

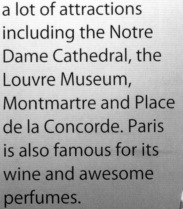

Eiffel Tower

Venice

Venice

Elegant Venetian buildings and palaces peer over the historical maze of narrow streets and labyrinth of canals that make this a unique city. Tourists naturally flock to Venice to experience its unmatched charm. A good way to get to know a more personal side of Venice is to saunter through its romantic back streets.

Rome and Vatican City

Rome is an ancient city in Italy which is famous for its culture and beautiful historical buildings. The Colosseum is probably the most ancient monument in Rome.

Rome is especially popular because of Vatican City. You can find there the most valuable pieces of art in the world. The Sistine chapel can be called the artistic jewel of Vatican City. You can walk there for hours admiring the beautiful frescoes of Michelangelo which are well-known worldwide. Some other beautiful places to visit in Rome are the Trevo Fontain and the Catacombs of Rome.

The Roman Colosseum

Another of the many interesting places to visit in Rome is the Roman Colosseum. This grand site was originally a huge amphitheatre that could seat more than 50,000 people. With amazing ancient architecture, even in disrepair, this is a magnificent site.

Colosseum

Vatican City

London

London is a beautiful city with many historical buildings. Buckingham Palace is a beautiful building in London and is the official Residence of the British monarch. Everyone can visit this palace and there are different galleries with beautiful art works from painters like Rubens, Van Eyck and many others. There are different galleries and you can also take a walk in the gardens and admire the beautiful flowers.

Other places of interest are the Tower of London, St. Paul's Cathedral, the Marble Arch near Hyde Park Corner and the Windsor Castle.

Edinburgh Castle

Edinburgh Castle is another interesting place to visit in Europe. It is over 1,000 years old and once you see this magnificent castle you'll soon understand why more than a million people visit it each year. You can tour the castle, enjoy the views and visit the surrounding gardens as well.

Tower Bridge

Since 1894, this beautifully designed bridge has been standing over the River Thames in the city of London. From the bridge's beautiful walkways you can see some breathtaking views of London. You can also visit the engine rooms containing the steam engines that power the bridge.

Big Ben

The world's largest turret clock tower, Big Ben is one of the best known landmarks in London and definitely one of the most interesting places to visit in Europe. Although, it is not open for public tours, it looks spectacular, especially at night when it is all lit up.

Hofburg Imperial Palace

Some other important places to visit are the palace of Shönbrunn with their beautiful gardens, the Wienerwald, the Donau Park, the St. Stephans Cathedral, the Karlskirche and Prater.

Johan Strauss

Vienna

Vienna, the capital of Austria, is the city of the classical music. There is a lovely park with a statue of Johan Strauss, the composer of 'The Blue Danube.' A statue of Mozart and images from Don Giovanna can be found in Burggarten. Also the Staatsoper and the Volksoper are popular places for music lovers.

You certainly need to visit the Hofburg Imperial Palace where you can visit the Sissi Museum.

Brussels

Brussels is the capital city of Belgium, but many also consider it the capital of the European Union. Though Brussels is the headquarters of both NATO and the European Union, you don't have to worry about being surrounded by just international diplomats. This beautiful city has several vibrant areas, such as Elsene, which is packed with restaurants and bars. Brussels is surrounded by parks and one of the coolest is the Cinquantenaire Park.

Cinquantenaire Park

Berlin

Berlin

Berlin has played a key role in several tragic historical events; it was the base for Hitler's Nazi army, the battleground of the cold war, and it was later divided by the Berlin Wall. Berlin remembers its past with several monuments and museums that are all worth seeing. Today Berlin is the heart of Germany and a wonderful and exciting city. people travelling to Berlin can enjoy trendy restaurants, shops, pubs and boutiques. Berlin has great public transportation, so you'll be able to get around the city easily. It is a popular tourist destination and for many students it is also a popular destination because of its festivals, urban charm and the fact that it has a busy rail hub.

Athens

Athens is more than just a city. It is the birthplace of modern civilization, the beginning of the creation of the west, and the start of democracy. The capital of Greece and a major metropolitan with 3.7 million citizens, this city offers a lot. A gorgeous skyline with many old and beautiful buildings, and ruins that date back to B.C., Athens is tourists delight! It's a great way to get the full feeling of Athens and see it through the eyes of the locals.

Acropolis

Acropolis

If you are interested in history, one historical site in Europe that you won't want to miss is the Acropolis at Athens. The term acropolis means **upper city**. The Acropolis is a flat-topped rock that rises 150 m above sea level in the city of Athens. Along with some other historical monuments stands the Parthenon, a temple dedicated to Goddess Athena, the protector of Athens. Apart from all this, the Acropolis offers an excellent view of Athens as well.

Leaning tower of Pisa

Santa Maria del Fiora

Prague

The Czech Republic's capital, Prague is one of the most popular destinations in Eastern Europe. Its attraction lies in the physical beauty of the city with 600 years old architecture amazingly untouched by war. The centre has been designated a UNESCO World Heritage Site and it demands to be explored on foot, an entire outdoor museum of history and a haphazard mixture of splendid architecture.

Tuscany

Tuscany is one of the most beautiful places in Italy situated in the east of the Liguarian Sea and the Tyrrhenian Sea. Florence and Siena are the two cities in Tuscany where you can find the most pieces of art. The

Duomo and the Cathedral are masterpieces and are well-known. The cathedral 'Santa Maria del Fiora' is the most important building in Florence.

The Leaning Tower of Pisa is also an important building in Tuscany and is popular worldwide. Many of Michelangelo's works can be found in Tuscany and especially in Florence. Almost everyone knows his most popular work 'David' which he created for the cathedral of Florence but the original work is now preserved in The Gallery of the Academia di Belle Arte.

David

Michelangelo's creation-David

27

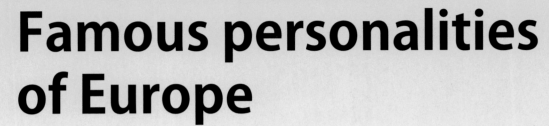

Famous personalities of Europe

Charlemagne

The Emperor Charlemagne may be considered as the 'Father of Europe'. He managed to consolidate a large part of Western Europe, and laid the principles of government which were later inherited by major European States. He was crowned Holy Roman Emperor in the year 88. He chose Aachen (a German city today) as the capital of his Empire.

Johannes Gutenberg

In 1440, German inventor Johannes Gutenberg invented a printing process with refinements and increased mechanization that remained the principal means of printing until the late 20th century. The inventor's method of printing from movable type, including the use of metal

moulds and alloys, a special press and oil-based inks, allowed for the first time the mass production of printed books.

Leonardo Da Vinci

Leonardo was a painter, sculptor, architect, musician, engineer, inventor and a scientist. He is most likely the epitome of the Renaissance man. Leonardo was also a great engineer and inventor. There were many instances where Leonardo was commissioned by the government to design elaborate state buildings or churches or to conceive new weapons that would surprise the enemy.

Not only was he a great inventor, Leonardo da Vinci was one of the greatest scientific minds ever to have lived. There are a massive number of observations and experiments that were executed and recorded in his sketches. Leonardo, before his death would have completed many studies of the human body. There are elaborate, detailed drawings of bone and muscle structure, organ-system observations and reproductive studies!

Galileo Galilee

The telescope was introduced to astronomy in 1609 by the great Italian scientist Galileo Galilee. He was the first man to see the craters of the moon, and who went on to discover sunspots, the four large moons of Jupiter, and the rings of Saturn.

Nicolaus Copernicus

Born to in a wealthy merchant family in Poland in 1473, Copernicus studied at university before becoming a canon of Frauenburg cathedral, a position he held for the rest of his life. Alongside his church duties he pursued an interest in astronomy, reintroducing the **heliocentric view** of the solar system, which means that the planets revolve around the sun. He died shortly after the first publication of his key work 'De revolutionibus orbium coelestium libri VI,' in 1543.

Isaac Newton

Born in England in 1642, Newton was one of the great figures of the scientific revolution, making major discoveries in optics, mathematics and physics, in which his three laws of motion form an underlying part. He was also active in the area of scientific philosophy, but was deeply hostile to criticism and was involved in several verbal feuds with other scientists. He died in 1727.

Charles Darwin

The father of arguably the most controversial scientific theory of the modern age, Darwin was born in England in 1809 and first made a name for himself as a geologist. He developed the famous theory of evolution of species. Also a naturalist, he arrived at a theory of evolution through the process of **Natural Selection**. This theory was published in 'On the Origin of Species' in 1859 and went on to gain widespread scientific acceptance as it was proved correct. He died in 1882, after winning many accolades.

Albert Einstein

Although Einstein became an American in 1940, he was born in Germany in 1879 and lived there until being driven out by the Nazis. He is without doubt the key figure of 20th century Physics, and probably the most iconic scientist of that era. He developed the Special and General Theory of Relativity and gave insights into space and time which are still being found true to this day. He died in 1955.

Beethoven

Ludwig van Beethoven was born in Bonn, Germany in 1770. Ludwig van Beethoven is one of the world's most famous and influential composers of classical music. His music has been played all over the world for over 180 years. Around 1796 Beethoven began to lose his hearing ability. Even then he continued to compose, conduct and perform music. By 1814 he was completely deaf.

Test Your MEMORY

1. What is the name given to the continuous mass of land formed by Asia and Europe?

2. Which place in Europe is regarded as the birthplace of the Western culture?

3. Which Italian scholar and poet first used the term 'the Dark Ages'?

4. What was Black Death?

5. Which invention of James Watt led to the beginning of the Industrial Revolution in Europe?

6. Name Europe's longest river?

7. How many states are members of the European Union?

8. Name the original six founding states of the European Union.

9. What is the name of the single currency of the European Union?

10. On which river is the Tower Bridge built?

11. Which Emperor is considered to be the 'Father of Europe'?

12. Who invented the printing press?

Index

* Maps not to scale; for illustration purpose only.